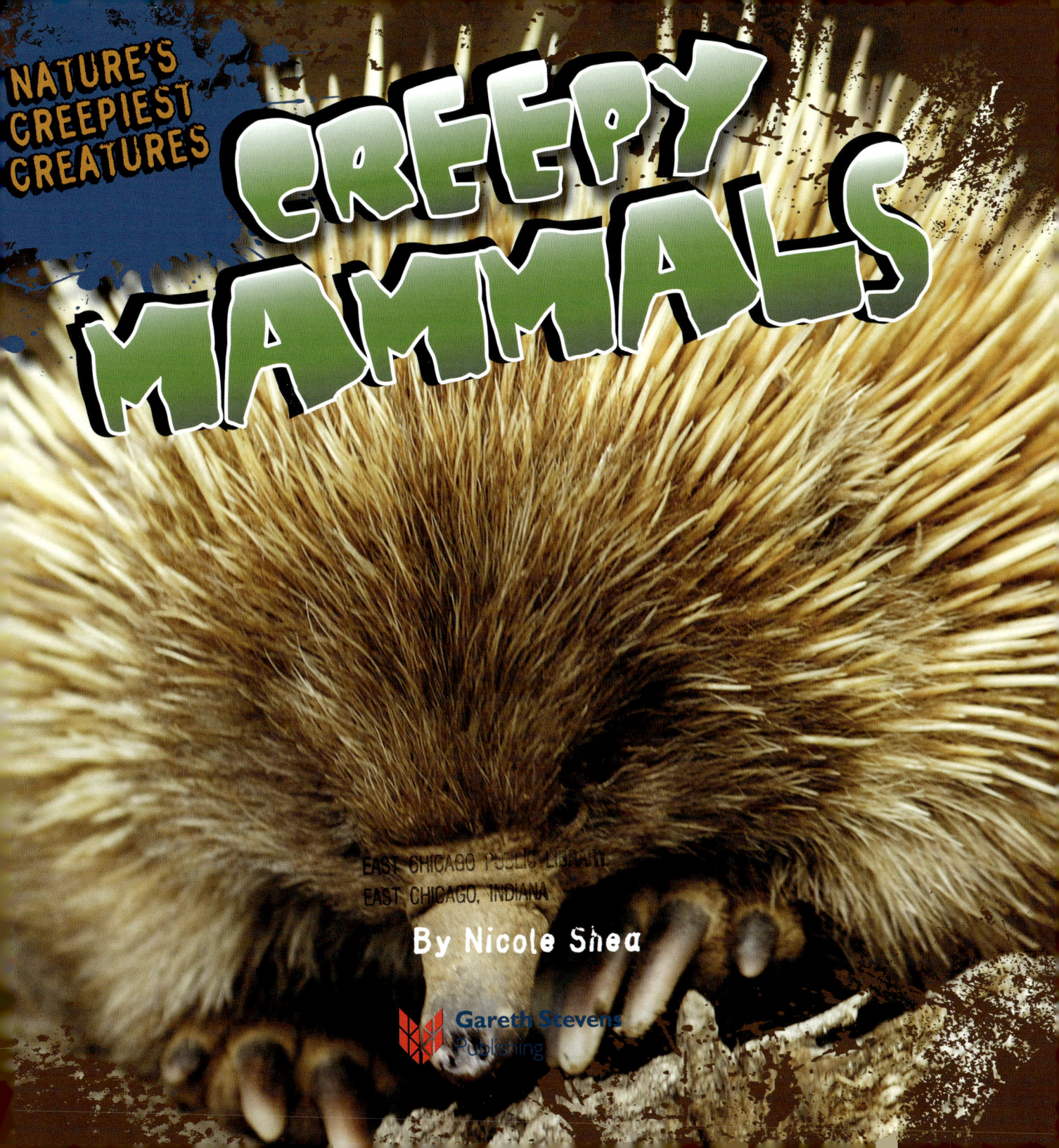

NATURE'S CREEPIEST CREATURES

CREEPY MAMMALS

By Nicole Shea

Gareth Stevens Publishing

Please visit our website, www.garethstevens.com. For a free color catalog of all our high-quality books, call toll free 1-800-542-2595 or fax 1-877-542-2596.

Library of Congress Cataloging-in-Publication Data

Shea, Nicole, 1976-
Creepy mammals / Nicole Shea.
    p. cm. — (Nature's creepiest creatures)
Includes index.
ISBN 978-1-4339-6495-4 (pbk.)
ISBN 978-1-4339-6496-1 (6-pack)
ISBN 978-1-4339-6493-0 (library binding)
1. Mammals—Juvenile literature. I. Title.
QL706.2.S46 2012
599—dc23
                                        2011031675

First Edition

Published in 2012 by
Gareth Stevens Publishing
111 East 14th Street, Suite 349
New York, NY 10003

Copyright © 2012 Gareth Stevens Publishing

Designer: Haley W. Harasymiw
Editor: Kristen Rajczak

Photo credits: Cover, pp. 1, 4-5, 6, 7, 8, 9, 10, 11, 13, 15, 19, 21 Shutterstock.com; p. 17 Neil Bromhall/Oxford Scientific/Getty Images.

All rights reserved. No part of this book may be reproduced in any form without permission in writing from the publisher, except by a reviewer.

Printed in the United States of America

CPSIA compliance information: Batch #CW12GS: For further information contact Gareth Stevens, New York, New York at 1-800-542-2595.

CONTENTS

Warm and Cuddly? 4

Real-Life Movie Monster 6

Seeing Red 8

Babirusa 10

Monotremes 12

Big Eyes 14

Life Underground 16

A Devilish Mammal 18

No Antlers Here 20

Glossary 22

For More Information 23

Index 24

Words in the glossary appear in **bold** type the first time they are used in the text.

Warm and Cuddly?

A mammal is a **warm-blooded** animal that has hair, gives birth to live babies, and feeds those babies milk from their mother's body. The largest living animal is a mammal. The blue whale can grow to be 100 feet (30 m) long!

Many of the animals we know best are mammals. Dogs, cats, and people are all mammals. However, some mammals can look or act strangely. Anteaters, for example, have a tube-shaped head and a tongue that can be more than 2 feet (61 cm) long!

FREAKY FACT:
A blue whale's heart can weigh as much as a car!

Anteaters use their sharp claws and strong legs to dig up ants and **termites** to eat.

Real-Life Movie Monster

Do you think vampires are only in the movies? The vampire bat drinks blood from animals and even humans! This bat is only about the size of your thumb, but it can drink half its weight in blood.

The vampire bat hunts at night. It creeps up on sleeping **prey** quietly, so it doesn't wake the prey up. Its nose can sense heat where the blood flows closest to the skin's surface. The bat then bites the animal and laps up its blood.

Freaky Fact:

A vampire bat's **saliva** keeps an animal's blood from thickening until the bat is done drinking.

Vampire bats drink blood mostly from birds, cows, pigs, and horses.

SEEING RED

Although this monkey looks like it's wearing an "angry mask," the bald uakari's red face isn't a sign of anger. It shows the monkey is healthy and happy!

Bald uakaris live in flooded forests along the Amazon River. They spend most of their time in trees. Bald uakaris have very strong jaws that they use to eat mostly seeds, fruit, and even nuts other animals can't break open.

FREAKY FACT:

Bald uakaris can move almost silently through the forest, even when traveling in big groups.

These mammals don't need a Halloween mask to look creepy!

BABIRUSA

Babirusa means "pig deer." The name is fitting since this mammal looks like a strange mix of a deer and a pig. Male babirusas have long teeth that grow out of their mouth and bend upward into **tusks**. As dangerous as they look, these tusks aren't for fighting. They guard the babirusa's eyes in battle. Babirusas fight with their long lower tusks, which they sharpen on trees. However, since they can weigh as much as 220 pounds (100 kg), babirusas have few enemies besides other babirusas!

FREAKY FACT:

A babirusa's curved tusks can grow so long they touch or even stab the animal's forehead.

This babirusa's teeth play an important part in its life.

MONOTREMES

Echidnas, whose bodies are covered in hair and **spines**, don't just look unusual. They also do an unusual thing for a mammal: they lay eggs! The only other mammal to lay eggs is the platypus. Echidnas and platypuses belong to a group of mammals called monotremes.

The female echidna lays one soft-shelled egg at a time. She carries it around in a pouch on her belly until the baby, called a puggle, hatches 10 days later. The puggle stays with its mother until its spines begin to grow about 7 weeks later.

FREAKY FACT:

Echidnas don't have teeth. They eat ants and termites with the help of a long, sticky tongue.

The echidna is an ancient animal. Scientists don't know much about its life in the wild.

13

Big Eyes

With their huge eyes, small body, short neck, and round head, tarsiers look as creepy as movie aliens!

Tarsiers can't move their big eyes, but they can turn their heads almost completely around to make up for it. Their large ears move to catch even the slightest sound. Tarsiers have long tails, long ankle bones, and special pads on their fingers. These help them hold on to branches and hunt insects, snakes, and birds by leaping from tree to tree.

FREAKY FACT:

A single eye of a tarsier weighs almost as much as its brain!

While tarsiers look a lot like monkeys, they're more like lemurs.

Life Underground

Naked mole-rats are strange mammals—and not just because they look totally hairless! These small mammals live underground in **colonies** that are much like those of bees.

Between 20 and 300 naked mole-rats live together in a system of tunnels. Each one has a job. A "queen" runs the colony and has babies. Other naked mole-rats are "soldiers." When a **predator**, such as a snake, comes into their tunnel home, the soldiers block the way. They use their long, sharp teeth to fight off the enemy!

FREAKY FACT:

The naked mole-rat's four front teeth are outside its mouth, and each of them can be moved independently!

Naked mole-rats aren't completely naked. They have about 100 fine hairs on their bodies that are used to feel what's around them.

A Devilish Mammal

Tasmanian devils are named for their wild anger and creepy, high-pitched screams. They're even noisier when fighting for food or the attention of a **mate**.

Devils travel up to 10 miles (16 km) each night to find food. They eat everything! Their strong jaws and teeth allow them to eat the bones of **carrion** and chew through metal traps. If that's not enough to keep you away, Tasmanian devils produce a smelly odor when they feel scared!

FREAKY FACT:

Tasmanian devils can have up to 50 young. However, the mother can only feed four. The babies have to fight each other for food.

Tasmanian devils have one of the strongest bites of any mammal.

NO ANTLERS HERE

The Chinese water deer, sometimes called a "vampire deer," isn't like the deer we see in fields. But don't worry, these deer only eat plants. They get their name from their scary-looking teeth.

A male water deer doesn't have antlers. Instead, its **canines** can reach a length of more than 3 inches (7.6 cm). They're not used to drink blood. The canines are often used to fight other males for territory and mates.

FREAKY FACT:
Chinese water deer bark when alarmed and scream when chased.

RECORD-BREAKING MAMMALS

smallest mammal	Bumblebee bats are only about 1.2 inches (3 cm) long.
tallest mammal	The tallest known giraffe was more than 19 feet (5.8 m) tall.
fastest land mammal	Cheetahs can run up to 70 miles (113 km) per hour, though only in short bursts.
heaviest land mammal	An African bush elephant weighed 20,000 pounds (9,080 kg).
longest life span	Some scientists think bowhead whales can live 200 years or more.

Glossary

canine: a long, pointed tooth near the front of the mouth

carrion: a dead animal

colony: a group of animals living together

mate: one of two animals that come together to produce babies

predator: an animal that hunts other animals for food

prey: an animal hunted by other animals for food

saliva: a watery matter animals make in their mouth to help break down food

spine: one of many stiff, pointed parts growing from an animal that are used for covering

termite: a small insect that eats wood

tusk: a large tooth that curves up and out of an animal's mouth

warm-blooded: able to keep the body at a steady temperature no matter what the outside temperature is

For More Information

Books

Gray, Susan Heinrichs. *The Life Cycle of Mammals.* Chicago, IL: Heinemann Library, 2012.

Taylor, Barbara. *The Mammal Book: Jaws, Paws, Claws and More.* London, England: Carlton Books, 2010.

Websites

Discovery Kids: Mammals
kids.discovery.com/tell-me/animals/mammals
Read more about different kinds of mammals.

Nat Geo Wild: Common Vampire Bat
animals.nationalgeographic.com/animals/mammals/common-vampire-bat/
Learn more about the vampire bat and look at pictures.

Smithsonian National Zoological Park: Mammals
nationalzoo.si.edu/Animals/SmallMammals/ForKids
Play games and read how you can help save animals all over the world.

Publisher's note to educators and parents: Our editors have carefully reviewed these websites to ensure that they are suitable for students. Many websites change frequently, however, and we cannot guarantee that a site's future contents will continue to meet our high standards of quality and educational value. Be advised that students should be closely supervised whenever they access the Internet.

Index

African bush elephant 21
Amazon River 8
anteaters 4, 5
babirusa 10, 11
bald uakari 8
blood 6, 7, 20
blue whale 4
bowhead whales 21
bumblebee bats 21
cheetahs 21
Chinese water deer 20
colonies 16
echidnas 12, 13
eggs 12
eyes 10, 14
giraffe 21
largest living animal 4
lemurs 15
monkey 8, 15
monotremes 12
naked mole-rats 16, 17
"pig deer" 10
platypus 12
predator 16
prey 6
puggle 12
queen 16
soldiers 16
tarsiers 14, 15
Tasmanian devils 18, 19
teeth 10, 11, 12, 16, 18, 20
tongue 4, 12
tusks 10
vampire bat 6, 7
"vampire deer" 20